Attack the Snails

Written by **Jan Burchett** and **Sara Vogler**

Illustrated by **Shahab Shamshirsaz**

OXFORD

UNIVERSITY PRESS

OXFORD
UNIVERSITY PRESS

Great Clarendon Street, Oxford, OX2 6DP, United Kingdom

Oxford University Press is a department of the University
of Oxford. It furthers the University's objective of excellence
in research, scholarship, and education by publishing
worldwide. Oxford is a registered trade mark of Oxford
University Press in the UK and in certain other countries

Text © Jan Burchett and Sara Vogler 2017
Illustrations © Shahab Shamshirsaz 2017
Inside cover notes written by Sam Keeley

British Library Cataloguing in Publication Data
Data available

ISBN: 978-0-19-841498-8

10 9 8 7 6 5 4 3 2 1

Paper used in the production of this book is a natural, recyclable product
made from wood grown in sustainable forests. The manufacturing process
conforms to the environmental regulations of the country of origin.

Printed in China by Golden Cup

Acknowledgements

Series Editor: Nikki Gamble

Meg grows peppers.

Dan grows flowers.

The trail stops.

Look at all
the snails!

A net might stop the snails.

But that night ...

Yum yum!

8

9

The flowers are growing.

Dan can pick them now.

It is all right, Dan. Bees are good for flowers!